THE
CONTEMPORARY
ENGLISH VERSION
(CEV)
An AntiChrist Version
(ACV)

By Pastor D. A. Waite, Th.D., Ph.D.
Director
Bible For Today, Inc.
900 Park Avenue
Collingswood, NJ 08108

PUBLISHED BY

THE BIBLE FOR TODAY PRESS
900 Park Avenue
Collingswood, NJ 08108
U.S.A.

Church Phone: 856-854-4747
BFT Phone: 856-854-4452
Orders: 1-800-John 10:9
Email: bft@BibleForToday.org
Website: www.BibleForToday.org
Fax: 856-854-2464

We Use and Defend
the King James Bible

September, 2008
BFT 2721

Copyright, 2008
All Rights Reserved
ISBN 1-56848-006-7

TABLE OF CONTENTS

THE CONTEMPORARY ENGLISH VERSION (CEV)
An AntiChrist Version (ACV)?

By Rev. D. A. Waite, Th.D. Ph.D.
Director, THE BIBLE FOR TODAY, INCORPORATED
900 Park Avenue, Collingswood, NJ 08108
Phone: 609-854-4452; FAX: 609-854-2464; Orders: 1-800-JOHN 10:9
E-Mail: BFT@Juno.Com

INTRODUCTORY COMMENTS

A. Method of Approach. An attempt was made to obtain the *Contemporary English Version* (CEV) on computer disk to better enable me to study the details of this translation. However, in calling the American Bible Society Customer Service line (1-800-322-4253) in November, 1996, I was informed that the CEV was not available in computer format. Because of this, I have had to "spot-check" some of the many words and verses referred to in this analysis without being able, due to time, to check them all. Had a computer version been available, I would have been able to get 100% accurate and final information in a matter of seconds.

Because of this, the statements made in this analysis are made on the basis of checking representative verses where the various terms occur. When I have not found the terms anywhere I looked, I have assumed (pending the CEV being available on a computer edition) that these terms do not occur anywhere throughout the CEV. The **nine** theological terms mentioned by the editors of the CEV as being dropped out of their version have been certainly eliminated. I assume the other terms not found in the places checked are also dropped out of the CEV.

B. An AntiChrist Version (ACV)? Why do I put in the subtitle of this analysis of the *Contemporary English Version (CEV)* **"An AntiChrist Version (ACV)?"** For **one reason**, neither the word **"Lucifer"** (Isaiah 14:12) nor the word **"AntiChrist"** occurs anywhere in the CEV. The word, **"AntiChrist"** (which is a transliteration of the Greek word, ἀντίχριστος) occurs in four verses in the New Testament. Here they are, in the King James Bible:

> **1 John 2:18** Little children, it is the last time: and as ye have heard that **antichrist** shall come, even now are there many **antichrists**; whereby we know that it is the last time.
> **1 John 2:22** Who is a liar but he that denieth that Jesus is the Christ? He is **antichrist**, that denieth the Father and the Son.

> **1 John 4:3** And every spirit that confesseth not that Jesus Christ is come in the flesh is not of God: and this is that **spirit of antichrist,** whereof ye have heard that it should come; and even now already is it in the world.

> **2 John 7** For many deceivers are entered into the world, who confess not that Jesus Christ is come in the flesh. This is a deceiver and an **antichrist.**

It is as though this version is seeking to HIDE the name of "AntiChrist" by eliminating it from their CEV. Another reason for my sub-title is found in 2 John 1:7-10:

> **2 John 1:7** For many deceivers are entered into the world, **who confess not that Jesus Christ is come in the flesh. This is a deceiver and an antichrist. 8** Look to yourselves, that we lose not those things which we have wrought, but that we receive a full reward.   **9** Whosoever transgresseth, and **abideth not in the doctrine of Christ**, hath not God. He that abideth in **the doctrine of Christ**, he hath both the Father and the Son.   **10** If there come any unto you, and **bring not this doctrine**, receive him not into your house, neither bid him God speed: **11** For he that biddeth him God speed is partaker of his evil deeds. (KJV)

Notice that the definition of an "AntiChrist" in verse 7 is those "**who confess not that Jesus Christ is come in the flesh.**" Since "**Christ is come in the flesh**" is NOT in the CEV, this version does not confess that doctrine in this verse, hence, by very definition of the New Testament, this version is "**a deceiver and an AntiChrist.**" A second item to note in this context is that when a person (or a version of the Bible, by application) "**abideth not in the doctrine of Christ,**" he doesn't have God, and if a person (or a version of the Bible, by application) "**brings not this doctrine,**" that is, the "**doctrine of Christ,**" you should "**receive him not into your house, neither bid him God speed. For he that biddeth him God speed is partaker of his evil deeds.**" By eliminating so many **doctrinal** words which concern the person and work of the Lord Jesus Christ, the CEV is not "**bringing the doctrine of Christ**" as it should be brought. I am referring to such doctrines as **(1) adoption, (2) imputation, (3) justification, (4) propitiation, (5) reconciliation, (6) repentance, (7) sanctification, (8) righteousness, (9) salvation** and others. There is no mention whatsoever of these and other vital doctrinal terms that concern our Lord Jesus Christ and His "doctrine." By using dynamic equivalent wording when speaking of the Greek words which convey these doctrines, they are either watering down such doctrines or are denying them completely to the English-speaking world. This is, by very definition of the Bible, the "spirit of AntiChrist." What is your own response to the phrase, "An AntiChrist Version (ACV)?"

I. THE CEV HAS THE WRONG HEBREW AND GREEK TEXTS:

A. The Wrong Hebrew Old Testament Text. According to the CEV *Preface*, the Hebrew Text used for the Old Testament was the *Biblia Hebraica Stuttgartensia* of the United Bible Societies. This is an erroneous Hebrew text as explained more in detail in my book, *Defending the King James Bible*, Chapter II (pages 20-38).

B. The Wrong Greek New Testament Text. The Greek Text used by the CEV was also published by the United Bible Societies. It was their 3rd edition, *"corrected and compared with the 4th revised edition"* [CEV *Preface*]. This is also an erroneous Greek text as explained more in detail in *Defending the King James Bible*, Chapter II (pages 38-62). The text based primarily on the corrupt text of Westcott and Hort who, in turn, based their text primarily on the still more corrupt uncial manuscripts of "B" (Vatican) and "Aleph" (Sinai). Further support of this considered opinion is found in *The Revision Revised* by Dean John William Burgon. This important and scholarly volume has just been reprinted in beautiful gold case-bound 640-page hardback format by the Dean Burgon Society. It is available as **B.F.T. #611** for a GIFT of **$25.00 + $5.00 P&H**. Dean Burgon's arguments against the false Greek text and theory of Westcott and Hort have been summarized in my own booklet entitled: *Westcott & Hort's Greek Text & Theory Refuted--Summarized from Dean Burgon's REVISION REVISED*. It is available as **B.F.T. #2695** for a GIFT of **$3.00 + $2.00 P & H**.

II. THE WRONG DOCTRINAL PHILOSOPHY OF "TRANSLATION"

There is a report entitled "AN EVALUATION OF THE CONTEMPÓRARY ENGLISH VERSION" given at the Dean Burgon Society's annual meeting on July 16, 1992. It was prepared and delivered by Dr. Robert Doom. Dr. Doom is the

President of the Russian Bible Society with headquarters in Asheville, North Carolina. It is available from the BIBLE FOR TODAY as **B.F.T. #2720** for a GIFT of **$1.50.** Our readers are urged to get a copy and read it. It is a helpful analysis of the CEV. Some of the quotations in this present booklet have been taken from this report.

In his evaluation, Dr. Doom analyzed the New Testament portion of the CEV which came out in 1991. The CEV was published by the American Bible Society (ABS) which had previously published the *Today's English Version* (TEV) also known as *Good News for Modern Man*. This came out in about 1976. Here is a quotation about the CEV taken from *Life Source: The Handbook for Life, Contemporary English Version* published by Thomas Nelson, 1991, from page iii:

> *"Traditional translations use words such as `justification,' `right-eousness,' `redemption,' `reconciliation,' `propitiation,' `atonement,' `salvation,' `sanctification,' and `repentance.'* ***All of these words are absent from the Contemporary English Version.""*** ["Introduction: Translating the CEV," p. iii]

As the chart on pages 8 and 9 indicates, the American Bible Society has done just that. Indeed, all of the above nine important doctrinal words have been eliminated from the CEV as well as 42 other words which have been used in the English speaking church-world for hundreds of years. The two reasons given by the ABS for eliminating these important doctrinal words were as follows:

> *"[1]* ***One reason for this absence [of these doctrinal words]*** *is that they are not used in everyday English."* [*Ibid,* p. iv] . . . [2] *But there is an even* ***more important reason***. *These are nouns, but they describe actions that God or people do. For example, the word `salvation' means `God saves people.' `Repentance' is more difficult, because it refers to more than event. Someone sinned and then turned from sin. In the CEV, each of these words may be translated in several different ways, depending on the special meaning they may have in a particular verse."* [*Ibid.,* p. iv]

By saying this, it is admitted that those who composed the CEV were "INTERPRETERS" rather than strictly and exclusively "TRANSLATORS"!

III. THE WRONG
INTERNATIONAL CONSEQUENCES

In his evaluation of the CEV, Dr. Doom (pages 2=3) quotes extensively from the Thomas Nelson Publisher's catalog advertising the CEV:

> *"Founded in 1816, the American Bible Society, was formed to spread the gospel and promote the distribution of the Holy Scriptures. Soon after its founding, the ABS took the Bible to the American frontier and began to unite with local Bible societies to reach and help immigrants, freed slaves, mariners, city youth, and minorities. Translation programs, begun in the 1800's, continue to bring the Scriptures to people of all cultures and races. As the American Bible Society celebrates its 175th anniversary, the ABS is launching a major effort to bring Bibles to Eastern Europe and the former Soviet Union.* **Overseas translations, publication, and distribution continues in partnership with Bible societies all over the world.**" [Thomas Nelson Catalog, Fall, 1992, page 49]

You can be certain that the BASIS for the English version to be used in the United Bible Societies **"all over the world"** will be this seriously flawed CONTEMPORARY ENGLISH VERSION (CEV). The CEV, therefore, has grave and dangerous international consequences.

IV. THE WRONG "TRANSLATION" OF VERSES

A. The Wrong "Translation" by PARAPHRASE and DYNAMIC EQUIVALENCY:

The examples given in this section demonstrate in small measure the liberties taken throughout the CEV by their use of paraphrase and dynamic equivalency. It is certainly not a "verbal equivalent" or a "form equivalent" work. It partakes of "dynamic equivalence" to an extent far greater than either the *New King James Version*, the *New American Standard Version*, or even the *New International Version*. For further information on "dynamic equivalence" dangers, the reader is referred to *Defending the King James Bible*, Chapter IV, pages 83-132.

1. Genesis 15:6 And he believed in the LORD; and **he counted it to him for righteousness.** (KJV)
    Genesis 15:6 Abram believed the LORD, and **the LORD was pleased_____ with him.** (CEV)
The whole concept of **"righteousness"** being counted or imputed to Abraham by faith is eliminated.

2. <u>Genesis 24:27</u> And he said, Blessed [be] the LORD God of my master
   Abraham, who hath not left destitute my master of his mercy and his truth:
   [being] in the way, the LORD led me to the house of my master's brethren.
   (KJV)
   Genesis 24:27 "I thank you, LORD God of my master Abraham! _____You
   have led me to his relatives and kept your promise to him."
   There is no mention of the **"LORD"** or of the servant's being **"in the way."**

3. <u>Psalm 1:1</u>   Blessed [is] the man that **walketh not** in the counsel of the ungodly,
   nor **standeth** in the way of sinners, nor **sitteth** in the seat of the scornful.
   (KJV)
   Psalm 1:1: God blesses those people who **refuse** evil advice and won't **follow**
   sinners or **join** in sneering at God. (CEV)
   The beautiful imagery of **"walking," "standing,"** and **"sitting"** has disappeared.

4. <u>Proverbs 22:6</u>   Train up a child **in the way he should go**: and when he is
   old, he will not depart from it. (KJV)
   Proverbs 22:6: Teach your children **right from wrong**, and when they are
   grown they will still do right. (CEV)
   "In the way he should go" includes far more than simply **"right from wrong."**

5. <u>Jeremiah 17:9</u> **The heart [is] deceitful** above all [things], and **desperately
   wicked**: who can know it? (KJV)
   Jeremiah 17:9 **You people of Judah are so deceitful** that you even fool
   yourselves and you can't change. (CEV)
   There is nothing said about the **"heart"** being **"deceitful"** nor is there any mention
   that the **"heart"** is **'desperately wicked."**

6. <u>Jeremiah 15:16</u> **Thy words** were found, and I did eat them; and thy word
   was unto me the **joy and rejoicing of mine heart**: for I am called by thy
   name, O LORD **God of hosts**. (KJV)
   Jeremiah 15:16 **When you spoke** to me **I was glad** to obey; because I belong
   to you, the LORD All-Powerful. (CEV)
   There is no mention of God's **"Words,"** nor of **"eating"** them, nor of considering
   them as **"the joy and rejoicing"** of his heart. The expression **"God of hosts"** (or
   armies) is entirely different from **"All-Powerful."**

7. <u>Daniel 1:8</u>   But Daniel **purposed in his heart** that he would not defile himself
   with the portion of the **king's meat**, nor with **the wine** which he drank: . . .
   (KJV)
   Daniel 1:8 Daniel **made up his mind** to eat and drink only what God had
   approved for his people to eat . . . (CEV)
   "Made up his mind" does not convey the depth of **"purposed in his heart."**

8. <u>Daniel 3:25</u> He answered and said, Lo, I see four men loose, walking in the midst of the fire, and they have no hurt; and the form of the fourth **is like the Son of God.** (KJV)
Daniel 3:25 . . . and the fourth one **looks like a god.** (CEV)
"Looks like a god" (with a small "g") is far different from **"IS like the Son of God"** (with a capital "G.")

9. <u>Zechariah 13:6</u> And [one] shall say unto him, What [are] **these wounds in thine hands?** Then he shall answer, [Those] with which I was wounded [in] the house of my friends. (KJV)
Zechariah 13:6 And if any of them are asked **why they are wounded,**_____
_____they will answer, "it happened at the house of some friends.
(CEV)
"Why they are wounded" is completely different from **"these wounds in thine hands"** which speaks prophetically of the Lord Jesus Christ's crucifixion.

10. <u>John 1:13</u> Which were born, **not of blood,** nor of the will of the flesh, nor of the will of man, but of God. (KJV)
John 1:13 They were not God's children by_____ **nature** or because of any human desires. God himself was the one who made them his children. (CEV)
"By nature" has no similarity in English to what the Greek says by **"not of blood."**

B. The Wrong "Translation" by Using the False Westcott and Hort Greek Text:

The following passages are just a few of the some 356 doctrinal passages where the false and REVISED GREEK TEXT of Westcott and Hort differs in error from the true RECEIVED GREEK TEXT that underlies the King James Bible. 158 of such passages are listed in Chapter V of my book, *Defending the King James Bible*, pages 133-187.

1. <u>Matthew 1:25</u> And knew her not till she had brought forth **her firstborn son:** and he called his name JESUS. (KJV)
Matthew 1:25 But they did not sleep together before her_____ **baby was** born. Then Joseph named him Jesus. (CEV)
By the elimination of **"firstborn,"** there is no assurance here of our Lord's Virgin Birth. Mary could have had many other children before Jesus was born. ⏌

2. <u>John 3:15</u> That whosoever believeth in **him should not perish,** but have eternal life. (KJV)
John 3:15 Then everyone who has faith in the <u>**Son of Man**</u>_____ **will**

have eternal life. (CEV)Acts 8:37
"**Son of Man**" is added to the text and "**should not perish**" (which speaks of hell and the Lake of Fire) is subtracted.

3. **Acts 8:37** And Philip said, If thou believest with all thine heart, thou mayest. And he answered and said, I believe that Jesus Christ is the Son of God. (KJV)
Acts 8:37 is entirely absent from the CEV.

4. **Romans 1:16** For I am not ashamed of **the gospel of Christ**: for it is the power of God unto **salvation** to every one that believeth; to the Jew first, and also to the Greek. (KJV)
Romans 1:16 I am proud of **the good news**_____. It is God's powerful way of saving all people who have faith whether they are Jews or Gentiles. (CEV)
The words, "**gospel**," "**salvation**," and the words, "**of Christ**," have been removed in this verse. In fact, "**gospel**" and "**salvation**" have also been eliminated throughout the CEV.

5. **1 Corinthians 5:7** Purge out therefore the old leaven, that ye may be a new lump, as ye are unleavened. For even Christ our passover is **sacrificed for us**: (KJV)
1 Corinthians 5:7 . . . Our Passover lamb is Christ who has already been **sacrificed**_____. (CEV)
The doctrine of the substitutionary death of Christ is eliminated here by the omission of the words, "**for us**."

6. **Mark 9:44** Where their worm dieth not, and the fire is not quenched. (KJV)
This verse is **not present in CEV.**

7. **Mark 9:46** Mark 9:46 Where their worm dieth not, and the fire is not quenched. (KJV)
This verse is **not present in CEV,**

8. **Matthew 18:11** For the Son of man is come to save that which was lost. (KJV)
This verse is **not present in CEV.**

9. **Luke 9:56** For the Son of man is not come to destroy men's lives, but to save [them]. And they went to another village. (KJV)
The first clause of this verse is **not present in CEV.**

10. **1 Corinthians 15:47** The first man [is] of the earth, earthy: **the second man** [is] the **Lord** from heaven. (KJV)

1 Corinthians 15:47 . . . but the **second man**_____ **came from heaven** (CEV)
The identification of Christ as "Lord" has disappeared.

11. <u>1 Timothy 3:16</u> And without controversy great is the mystery of godliness: **God was manifest in the flesh,** justified in the Spirit, seen of angels, preached unto the Gentiles, believed on in the world, received up into glory. (KJV)
    1 Timothy 3:16 . . . **Christ**_____ **came as a human** . . . (CEV)
The word must be "God" in this part of the verse. The word, "Christ" has been placed there without textual warrant of any kind. The Deity of Christ is questioned here as well as His Incarnation. "God" was manifest in the flesh!

12. <u>1 John 4:3</u> And every spirit that confesseth not that Jesus **<u>Christ is come in the flesh</u>** is not of God: and this is that [spirit] of **antichrist,** whereof ye have heard that it should come; and even now already is it in the world. (KJV)
    1 John 4:3 But when someone doesn't say this about **Jesus,**_____
    _____you know that person has a spirit that doesn't come from God and is the **enemy** of Christ. You know that this **enemy** was coming into the world and now is already here. (CEV)
By the elimination of **"Christ is come in the flesh,"** the false Westcott and Hort Greek text (as well as the CEV) has denied His incarnation once again. The CEV also does away with the term **"AntiChrist"** here and throughout its version.

13. <u>Ephesians 3:9</u> And to make all [men] see what [is] the fellowship of the mystery, which from the beginning of the world hath been hid in God, who created all things **by Jesus Christ:** (KJV)
    Ephesians 3:9 God, who created everything_____, wanted me to help everyone understand the mysterious plan that had always been hidden in his mind. (CEV)
By eliminating the three words, **"by Jesus Christ,"** the CEV, following the false Westcott and Hort Greek text, has not properly stated here that the Lord Jesus Christ was the Creator of **"all things."**

14. <u>2 Corinthians 4:14</u> Knowing that he which raised up the Lord Jesus shall raise up us also **<u>by</u>** Jesus, and shall present [us] with you. (KJV)
    2 Corinthians 4:14 Because we know that God raised the Lord Jesus to life. And just as God caused Jesus, he will also raise us_____ to life together with you. (CEV)
Omitting the preposition "by," and the entire expression, "by Jesus," removes the clear teaching of this verse . It is the Lord Jesus Christ Who is the member of the Godhead Who will raise up with resurrected bodies all of the believers who have died. The CEV says nothing about this important doctrinal truth.

15. <u>Colossians 1:14</u> In whom we have redemption **through his blood,** [even] the forgiveness of sins: (KJV)

Colossians 1:14 Who forgives ours sins_____ and sets us free. (CEV)
The CEV here has eliminated the truth that **"redemption"** has been made possible **"through His Blood,"** that is the Blood of the Lord Jesus Christ. In addition, the entire theological concept of **"redemption"** has disappeared.

16. <u>Hebrews 1:3</u> Who being the brightness of [his] glory, and the express image of his person, and upholding all things by the word of his power, when he had **by himself** purged our sins, sat down on the right hand of the Majesty on high; (KJV)

Hebrews 1:3 After the Son had_____ washed away our sins, he sat down at the right side of the glorious God in heaven. (CEV)
"By Himself" indicates that the Lord Jesus Christ ALONE purged our sins without the help of any other person or thing, including priests, sacraments, penance, purgatory, or any other additive.

IV. THE WRONG DOCTRINES AND WORDS ELIMINATED

The following are some of the words and doctrines that are absent from the CEV. This is based on a preliminary study based on spot-checking of the various verses in the KJB that contain such terms. When the CEV can be obtained on computer disk, the final tabulation can be made with absolute numbers. I could not find anywhere (in the passages checked) in the CEV the following words, many of which are doctrinal in nature. This includes the word indicated plus most if not all of its compounds:

The following **CHART** illustrates the number of times the word is used in the King James Bible (KJB), the *New International Version* (NIV), the *New Century Version* (NCV), and an estimate based on looking at a number of references in the *Contemporary English Version* (CEV). The *New Century Version* (NCV) is published by Word books and is almost as defective as the CEV, but not quite, as the **CHART** indicates in some of the words.

Doctrinal Words Changed or Discarded
The King James Bible (KJB)
The New International Version (NIV)
The New Century Version (NCV)
The Contemporary English Version (CEV)

DOCTRINAL TERM (+ COMPOUNDS)	KJB FREQ.	NIV FREQ.	NCV FREQ.	CEV `FREQ
*adoption	5	2	0	0
*Advocate (Christ)	1	0	0	0
*cleanse	32	20	6	0
*gospel	95	91	2	0
*grace	150	123	106	0
*impute	3	0	0	0
*judgment	285	128	38	0
*justification	3	2	0	0
*justify	11	7	0	0
*mercy	261	121	175	0
*mercy seat	27	0	1	0
*only begotten	6	0	0	0
*perish	118	82	0	0
*propitiation	3	0	0	0
*reconcile	5	3	0	0
*reconciliation	8	4	0	0
*redeem	40	44	0	0
*redemption	20	23	0	0
*repent	43	38	0	0
*repentance	26	21	0	0
*righteous	225	284	2	0
*righteousness	285	230	0	0
*saints	94	68	1	0

*salvation	150	118	67	0
*sanctification	6	0	0	0
*sanctify	65	4	0	0
*unrighteous	9	4	0	0
*unrighteousness	20	3	0	0
*vail (temple)	35	0	0	0
abide	77	0	0	0
abiding	55	0	0	0
carnal	15	0	0	0
chaste	3	0	0	0
chasten	46	2	0	0
concupiscence	3	0	0	0
covet	7	8	0	0
covetous	9	1	0	0
covetousness	19	0	0	0
filthy	16	5	5	0
firstfruits	30	29	3	0
flesh	148	34	38	0
fornication	44	0	0	0
lust	18	13	0	0
ordained	35	15	0	0
purge	15	16	0	0
reckon	8	0	0	0
seed (children)	254	75	0	0
sodomites	5	0	0	0
tribulation	22	1	0	0
ungodly	24	15	0	0
walk (figurative)	203	133	111	0

These fifty-one words are given in alphabetical order in two sections. The section with the asterisk [*] before each word (*adoption--*vail) is a section which contains the 29 words of the greatest doctrinal usage. The remaining 22 words (abide--walk) are samples of other words of general interest and usage. All of the above words (to the best of our sampling process) are words that are NOT found in the CEV.

VI. THE WRONG RESULTS IF THE CEV WERE ADOPTED

The world of the CEV and the world of the King James Bible are two separate and distinct worlds. The theology of the two is far different. Those who read and understand the King James Bible and its terms cannot communicate spiritual and theological verities with those who know **only** the CEV. They are poles apart because the CEV removed so many important and valuable theological terms.

If the CEV ever succeeds in taking over in "Christendom," the following might be undertaken at once:

1. There might be all new hymnals constructed with revised words.
2. There might be all new theology books written with revised words.
3. The old hymnals might be destroyed with their old words.
4. The old theology books might be destroyed with their old words.
   a. This would include the Protestant theology books of Hodge, Shedd, Robertson, Finney, Chafer, Bancroft, Strong, Buswell, and many others.
   b. This would include all Roman Catholic theologies as well, since they include many of these theological terms.

It is truly a REVOLUTIONARY bible version!! It should be exposed for what it is. It is much, much worse than the *Today's English Version (TEV)* known as *Good News for Modern Man.* even though the CEV includes the "blood of Christ" in 1 Peter 1:18-19. The TEV does not.

VII. THE WRONG UNDERSTANDING OF DOCTRINES

Since the terms in **bold face type** in the following verses do not appear in the CEV, it would seem that there would eventually come a great and fixed chasm of understanding of Bible doctrine between those using the King James Bible and those using the CEV. Here are a few verses which, among many others, would pose problems of comprehension to those brought up on the CEV:

1. Colossians 1:20 And, having made peace through the blood of his cross, by him

to **reconcile** all things unto himself; by him, [I say], whether [they be] things in earth, or things in heaven. (KJV)

"**Reconcile**" does not appear in the CEV.

2. Romans 8:15 For ye have not received the spirit of bondage again to fear; but ye have received the Spirit of **adoption**, whereby we cry, Abba, Father. (KJV)

"**Adoption**" does not appear in the CEV.

3. 1 Corinthians 5:7 **Purge** out therefore the old leaven, that ye may be a new lump, as ye are unleavened. For even Christ our passover is sacrificed **for us**: (KJV)

"**Purge**" does not appear in the CEV and "**for us**" does not appear in this verse.

4. Romans 3:30 Seeing [it is] one God, which **shall justify** the circumcision by faith, and uncircumcision through faith. (KJV)

"**Justify**" does not appear in the CEV.

5. Romans 5:1 Therefore **being justified** by faith, we have peace with God through our Lord Jesus Christ: (KJV)

"**Justify**" and "**justified**" do not appear in the CEV.

6. Ephesians 2:8-9 For by **grace** are ye saved through faith; and that not of yourselves: [it is] the gift of God: 9 Not of works, lest any man should boast. (KJV)

"**Grace**" does not appear in the CEV.

7. 1 Corinthians 1:30 But of him are ye in Christ Jesus, who of God is made unto us wisdom, and **righteousness**, and **sanctification**, and **redemption**: (KJV)

"**Righteousness**," "**sanctification**" and "**redemption**" do not appear in the CEV.

8. Exodus 20:17 Thou **shalt not covet** thy neighbour's house, thou **shalt not covet** thy neighbour's wife, nor his manservant, nor his maidservant, nor his ox, nor his ass, nor any thing that [is] thy neighbour's. (KJV)

"**Covet**" does not appear in the CEV.

9. Romans 7:7 What shall we say then? [Is] the law sin? God forbid. Nay, I had not known sin, but by the law: for I had not known lust, except the law had said, Thou **shalt not covet**. (KJV)

"**Covet**" does not appear in the CEV.

10. John 17:17 **Sanctify** them through thy truth: thy word is truth. (KJV)

"**Sanctify**" does not appear in the CEV.

11. 1 Thessalonians 5:23   And the very God of peace **sanctify** you wholly; and [I pray God] your whole spirit and soul and body be preserved blameless unto the coming of our Lord Jesus Christ. (KJV)
   "**Sanctify**" does not appear in the CEV.

12. Titus 2:11   For the **grace** of God that bringeth **salvation** hath appeared to all men, (KJV)
   "**Grace**" does not appear in the CEV.

13. Matthew 24:21 For then shall be **great tribulation,** such as was not since the beginning of the world to this time, no, nor ever shall be. (KJV)
   "**Tribulation**" does not appear in the CEV.

14. Proverbs 19:18   **Chasten** thy son while there is hope, and let not thy soul spare for his crying. (KJV)
   "**Chasten**" does not appear in the CEV.

15. 1 John 2:1   My little children, these things write I unto you, that ye sin not. And if any man sin, we have an **advocate** with the Father, Jesus Christ the righteous: (KJV)
   "**Advocate**" does not appear in the CEV.

16. 2 Corinthians 11:2   For I am jealous over you with godly jealousy: for I have espoused you to one husband, that I may present [you as] a **chaste** virgin to Christ. (KJV)
   "**Chaste**" does not appear in the CEV.

17. 1 Kings 14:24 And there were also **sodomites** in the land: [and] they did according to all the abominations of the nations which the LORD cast out before the children of Israel. (KJV)
   The word, "**sodomites,**" does not appear in the CEV.

18. Romans 4:8 Blessed [is] the man to whom the Lord will not **impute** sin. (KJV)
   "**Impute**" does not appear in the CEV.

19. 1 Corinthians 3:3 For ye are yet **carnal:** for whereas [there is] among you envying, and strife, and divisions, are ye not **carnal,** and walk as men? (KJV)
   "**Carnal**" does not appear in the CEV.

20. Mark 15:38   And the **veil** of the temple was rent in twain from the top to the bottom. (KJV)
   "**Veil**" in the sense of the "veil/vail of the temple" does not appear in the CEV.

21. Romans 1:29 Being filled with all **unrighteousness, fornication,** wickedness, **covetousness,** maliciousness; full of envy, murder, debate, deceit, malignity; whisperers, (KJV)

"**Unrighteousness,**" "**fornication,**" and "**covetousness**" do not appears in the CEV.

22. John 5:38 And ye have not his word **abiding** in you: for whom he hath sent, him ye believe not. (KJV)

"**Abiding**" does not appear in the CEV.

23. John 15:4 **Abide** in me, and I in you. As the branch cannot bear fruit of itself, except it **abide** in the vine; no more can ye, except ye **abide** in me. (KJV)

"**Abide**" does not appear in the CEV.

24. Exodus 25:22 And there I will meet with thee, and I will commune with thee from above the **mercy seat,** from between the two cherubims which [are] upon the ark of the testimony, of all [things] which I will give thee in commandment unto the children of Israel. (KJV)

"**Mercy seat**" does not appear in the CEV.

25. Revelation 2:5 Remember therefore from whence thou art fallen, and **repent,** and do the first works; or else I will come unto thee quickly, and will remove thy candlestick out of his place, except thou **repent.** (KJV)

"**Repent**" does not appear in the CEV.

26. Acts 20:21 Testifying both to the Jews, and also to the Greeks, **repentance** toward God, and faith toward our Lord Jesus Christ. (KJV)

"**Repentance**" does not appear in the CEV.

27. Romans 4:5 But to him that worketh not, but believeth on him that **justifieth** the **ungodly,** his faith is counted for **righteousness.** (KJV)

"**Justifieth**"(or "**justifies**"), "**ungodly,**" and "**righteousness**" do not appear in the CEV.

28. Romans 10:10 For with the heart man believeth unto **righteousness**; and with the mouth **confession** is made unto **salvation.** (KJV)

"**Righteousness,**" "**confession,**" and "**salvation**" do not appear in the CEV.

29. 2 Corinthians 6:14 Be ye not unequally yoked together with unbelievers: for what fellowship hath **righteousness** with **unrighteousness**? and what **communion** hath light with darkness? (KJV)

"**Righteousness,**" "**unrighteousness,**" and "**communion**" do not appear in the CEV.

30. <u>Ephesians 1:7</u> In whom we have **redemption** through his blood, the for-giveness of sins, according to the riches of his **grace**; (KJV)
"**Redemption**" and "**grace**" do not appear in the CEV.

31. <u>Romans 3:25</u> Whom God hath set forth [to be] a **propitiation** through faith in his blood, to declare his **righteousness** for the **remission** of sins that are past, through the forbearance of God; (KJV)
"**Propitiation**," "**righteousness**" and "**remission**" do not appear in the CEV.

32. <u>2 Corinthians 5:19</u> To wit, that God was in Christ, **reconciling** the world unto himself, not **imputing** their **trespasses** unto them; and hath committed unto us the word of **reconciliation**. (KJV)
"**Reconciling**," "**imputing**," "**trespasses**," and "**reconciliation**" do not appear in the CEV.

33. <u>Romans 5:18</u> Therefore as by the offence of one [judgment came] upon all men to condemnation; even so by the **righteousness** of one [the free gift came] upon all men unto **justification** of life. (KJV)
"**Righteousness**" and "**justification**" do not appear in the CEV.

34. <u>Romans 5:16</u> And not as [it was] by one that sinned, [so is] the gift: for the judgment [was] by one to **condemnation**, but the free gift [is] of many offences unto **justification**. (KJV)
"**Condemnation**" and "**justification**" do not appear in the CEV.

35. <u>Romans 1:16</u> For I am not ashamed of the **gospel** of Christ: for it is the power of God unto **salvation** to every one that believeth; to the Jew first, and also to the Greek. (KJV)
"**Gospel**" and "**salvation**" do not appear in the CEV.

VIII. THE WRONG WAY OF SALVATION

In the CEV, on page 1354 in the paperback edition that I have, there is a section entitled, "**WHAT THE BIBLE SAYS ABOUT GOD'S FORGIVE-NESS.**" When this half-page of words is read closely and carefully, it ends up as a **wrong (or at least an unclear) way of salvation.** Each of the five points has some Scripture verses underneath them. Here are the five points:
1. "Every person is separated from God because of sin." This is true.

2. "God has always sought to form a close relationship with people." This is true.
3. "God has reached out to people in a personal way by sending Jesus Christ." This is true, but He can't help those who reject Him!
4, **"God's forgiveness through Jesus Christ is available to every person."** This is subject to interpretation. Do the words **"available to every person"** mean that **"every person"** <u>HAS</u> **"God's forgiveness"**? This sentence is subject to various interpretations and even misinterpretations. It is capable of being taken in two different and opposite ways. It might be teaching "universalism," that is, each and every person in the world (**"every person"**) has **"God's forgiveness"** because **"Jesus Christ"** was sent into the world. Notice, they do NOT say: **"God's forgiveness is available to every person THROUGH JESUS CHRIST."** That might mean that each person would have to come **"through Jesus Christ"** in order to receive **"God's forgiveness."** This is true. Are they purposely vague?

If you read through the verses that are listed under this point, you do not find any mention of the **consequences** of rejecting faith in the Lord Jesus Christ as Savior and Lord. It would appear that the ABS's use of the word **"available"** is used to mean that **"every person"** <u>HAS</u> **"God's forgiveness"**! If I have a new car **"available"** to me, I have the use of it and it is my own to do with as I see fit. In the case of God's **"forgiveness"** is concerned, it is NOT **"available"** to the lost person who refuses to accept the Lord Jesus Christ as their Savior. Why don't they make it clear, as the Bible does, that **"God's forgiveness"** is predicated solely upon the individual's personal and genuine **faith** in the Lord Jesus Christ? **The only verses that come close are Romans 10:9 and 13, and Romans 3:22, 24, and 26, <u>IF</u> they are explained clearly.** Why don't they use John 3:16?

John 3:16 For God so loved the world, that he gave his only begotten Son, that whosoever believeth in him **should not perish**, but have everlasting life. (KJV)

► Why don't they use John 3:18?

John 3:18 He that believeth on him is not condemned: but **he that believeth not is condemned already**, because he hath not believed in the name of the only begotten Son of God. (KJV)

► Why don't they use John 3:36?

John 3:36 He that believeth on the Son hath everlasting life: and **he that believeth not the Son shall not see life; but the wrath of God abideth on him.** (KJV)

► Why don't they use Romans 4:5?

Romans 4:5 But to him that worketh not, but believeth on him that justifieth the ungodly, **his faith is counted for righteousness.** (KJV)

► Why don't they use Romans 5:1?

Romans 5:1   Therefore being **justified by faith,** we have peace with God through our Lord Jesus Christ: (KJV)

►Why don't they use Ephesians 2:8-9?

Ephesians 2:8-9 For by grace are ye saved **through faith**; and that not of yourselves: [it is] the gift of God: 9 Not of works, lest any man should boast. (KJV)

Here are the verses whose references are listed by the American Bible Society to corroborate point #4. I have printed them in full from the King James Bible:

Psalm 51:1-17: 1. Have mercy upon me, O God, according to thy lovingkindness: according unto the multitude of thy tender mercies blot out my transgressions. 2. Wash me throughly from mine iniquity, and cleanse me from my sin. 3 For I acknowledge my transgressions: and my sin [is] ever before me. 4 Against thee, thee only, have I sinned, and done [this] evil in thy sight: that thou mightest be justified when thou speakest, [and] be clear when thou judgest. 5 Behold, I was shapen in iniquity; and in sin did my mother conceive me. 6 Behold, thou desirest truth in the inward parts: and in the hidden [part] thou shalt make me to know wisdom. 7 Purge me with hyssop, and I shall be clean: wash me, and I shall be whiter than snow. 8 Make me to hear joy and gladness; [that] the bones [which] thou hast broken may rejoice. 9 Hide thy face from my sins, and blot out all mine iniquities. 10 Create in me a clean heart, O God; and renew a right spirit within me. 11 Cast me not away from thy presence; and take not thy holy spirit from me. 12 Restore unto me the joy of thy salvation; and uphold me [with thy] free spirit. 13 [Then] will I teach transgressors thy ways; and sinners shall be converted unto thee. 14 Deliver me from bloodguiltiness, O God, thou God of my salvation: [and] my tongue shall sing aloud of thy righteousness. 15 O Lord, open thou my lips; and my mouth shall shew forth thy praise. 16 For thou desirest not sacrifice; else would I give [it]: thou delightest not in burnt offering. 17 The sacrifices of God [are] a broken spirit: a broken and a contrite heart, O God, thou wilt not despise. (KJV) [**This forgiveness is "available" to and restricted ONLY for believers, NOT for "every person"**!]

1 John 1:5-10: 5.This then is the message which we have heard of him, and declare unto you, that God is light, and in him is no darkness at all. 6. If we say that we have fellowship with him, and walk in darkness, we lie, and do not the truth: 7 But if we walk in the light, as he is in the light, we have fellowship one with another, and the blood of Jesus Christ his Son cleanseth us from all sin. 8 If we say that we have no sin, we deceive ourselves, and the truth is not in us. 9 If we confess our sins, he is faithful and just to forgive us [our] sins, and to cleanse us from all unrighteousness. 10 If we say that we have not sinned, we make him a liar, and his word is not in us. (KJV) [**Again, this forgiveness is "available" to and restricted ONLY for believing, born again Christians, NOT for "every person"**!]

Romans 10:5-13: 5 For Moses describeth the righteousness which is of the law, That the man which doeth those things shall live by them. 6. But the righteousness which is of faith speaketh on this wise, Say not in thine heart, Who shall ascend into heaven? (that is, to bring Christ down [from above]:) 7 Or, Who shall descend into the deep? (that is, to bring up Christ again from the dead.) 8 But what saith it? The word is nigh thee, [even] in thy mouth, and in thy heart: that is, the word of faith, which we preach; **9 That if thou shalt confess with thy mouth the Lord Jesus, and shalt believe in thine heart that God hath raised him from the dead, thou shalt be saved. 10 For with the heart man believeth unto righteousness; and with the mouth confession is made unto salvation.** 11 For the scripture saith, Whosoever believeth on him shall not be ashamed. 12 For there is no difference between the Jew and the Greek: for the same Lord over all is rich unto all that call upon him. **13 For whosoever shall call upon the name of the Lord shall be saved.** (KJV) [**Again, this forgiveness is "available" to and restricted ONLY for believing, born again Christians, NOT for "every person"**!]

Psalm 32:1-11: 1 Blessed [is he whose] transgression [is] forgiven, [whose] sin [is] covered. 2. Blessed [is] the man unto whom the LORD imputeth not iniquity, and in whose spirit [there is] no guile. 3 When I kept silence, my bones waxed old through my roaring all the day long. 4 For day and night thy hand was heavy upon me: my moisture is turned into the drought of summer. Selah. 5 I acknowledged my sin unto thee, and mine iniquity have I not hid. I said, I will confess my transgressions unto the LORD; and thou forgavest the iniquity of my sin. Selah. 6 For this shall every one that is godly pray unto thee in a time when thou mayest be found: surely in the floods of great waters they shall not come nigh unto him. 7 Thou [art] my hiding place; thou shalt preserve me from trouble; thou shalt compass me about with songs of deliverance. Selah. 8 I will instruct thee and teach thee in the way which thou shalt go: I will guide thee with mine eye. 9 Be ye not as the horse, [or] as the mule, [which] have no understanding: whose mouth must be held in with bit and bridle, lest they come near unto thee. 10 Many sorrows [shall be] to the wicked: but he that trusteth in the LORD, mercy shall compass him about. 11 Be glad in the LORD, and rejoice, ye righteous: and shout for joy, all [ye that are] upright in heart. (KJV) [**This forgiveness is "available" to and restricted ONLY for believers, NOT for "every person"**!]

Romans 8:31-39: 31. What shall we then say to these things? If God [be] for us, who [can be] against us? 32. He that spared not his own Son, but delivered him up for us all, how shall he not with him also freely give us all things? 33 Who shall lay any thing to the charge of God's elect? [It is] God that justifieth. 34 Who [is] he that condemneth? [It is] Christ that died, yea rather, that is risen again, who is even at the right hand of God, who also maketh intercession for us. 35 Who shall separate us from the love of Christ? [shall] tribulation, or distress, or persecution, or famine, or nakedness, or peril, or sword? 36 As it is written, For thy sake we are killed all the day long; we are accounted as sheep for the slaughter. 37 Nay, in all these things we are more than conquerors through him that loved us. 38 For I am persuaded, that neither death, nor life, nor angels, nor principalities, nor powers, nor things present, nor things to come, 39 Nor height, nor depth, nor any other creature, shall be able to separate us from the love of God, which is in Christ Jesus our Lord. (KJV) [**Again, this forgiveness is "available" to and restricted ONLY for believing, born again Christians, NOT for "every person"!**]

Romans 3:21-26: 21. But now the righteousness of God without the law is manifested, being witnessed by the law and the prophets;   22. Even the righteousness of God [which is] by faith of Jesus Christ unto all and upon all them that believe: for there is no difference: 23 For all have sinned, and come short of the glory of God; **24 Being justified freely by his grace through the redemption that is in Christ Jesus:** 25 Whom God hath set forth [to be] a propitiation through faith in his blood, to declare his righteousness for the remission of sins that are past, through the forbearance of God; **26 To declare, [I say], at this time his righteousness: that he might be just, and the justifier of him which believeth in Jesus.** (KJV) [**Again, this forgiveness is "available" to and restricted ONLY for believing, born again Christians, NOT for "every person"!**]

5.   "New life in Christ calls a person to live in a Christ-like way." This is true but you must be "saved" and "regenerated" first!

CONCLUSION

It is indeed sad that the American Bible Society has come out with this *Contemporary English Version (CEV)*. From every possible point of view, it is a defective piece of work. Its damage in the years and decades to come will be incalculable. It is only hoped that its days may be few, and its readers still fewer! As for me and my house, we will continue to honor the King James Bible with all of its important and theologically correct theological terminology. It is a Bible in which we can place our confidence. It has superior Hebrew and Greek TEXTS. It has superior TRANSLATORS. It has superior TECHNIQUE of translation. It has superior THEOLOGY. For further proofs of this four-fold superiority, why not order a copy of our book, *Defending the King James Bible*.

INDEX OF TERMS

INDEX OF SCRIPTURE REFERENCES

APPENDICES

QUESTIONS AND ANSWERS ON THE SUBJECT OF "DEFENDING THE KING JAMES BIBLE-- GOD'S WORDS KEPT INTACT IN ENGLISH"

The following questions and answers are only a few examples from the book *Defending the King James Bible, A Fourfold Superiority* by Pastor D. A. Waite, Th.D., Ph.D. This work is now a classic and would be a valuable addition to any library. The book may be ordered from:

www.biblefortoday.org
1-800-JOHN 10:9

1. WHAT GREEK TEXTS WERE USED BEFORE PRINTED TEXTS?

Q. You said that Beza's text came out in 1598. What did they use before that?

A. They used the manuscripts they had copied. The manuscripts were handwritten, not in printed form, being copies of copies, beginning with the original Greek New Testament writings. The first printed form of the Received Text was that of Erasmus in 1516. In the preface to the Trinitarian Bible Society's Greek New Testament there is a history of the text. It mentions there that Desiderius Erasmus printed the text in 1516. Erasmus was a Roman Catholic. A lot of people who follow Westcott and Hort like to say, "Well, Erasmus was a Roman Catholic and he was no good; therefore, we shouldn't follow his text." They say he was a Humanist and therefore bad. Well, he was a Humanist, but not like the Humanists of Secular Humanism today. He believed the Bible. He believed it was God's Word. He wanted people to read it in the Greek text in which it was originally written, not just in the Latin Vulgate that most people had. In his day, Erasmus was the greatest Greek scholar on the European continent. He was the one everyone looked to, and under whom they wanted to study. A number of people studied Greek under Erasmus. He was the one who gave the Greek pronunciation we still use today.

In 1516, Erasmus' Greek New Testament came out in the first edition. He had many other editions. Martin Luther used one of

Erasmus' editions for his German translation. The Complutensian Polyglot was edited by Cardinal Ximenes and was published in Acala, Spain. It was called a "polyglot" because it contained a number of languages in addition to the Greek. That was printed in 1514, but wasn't circulated until 1522. Actually the first Greek New Testament to be printed was the Complutensian Polyglot. Erasmus' edition came out in 1516. Once the printing press got into use, the changes were not as great, because the editions would be type-set. Before that, they just had to use handwritten manuscripts.

2.   IS IT DIFFICULT TO RENDER THE HEBREW EXACTLY INTO ENGLISH?

Q.   **Is it difficult to make the Hebrew exact into English?**

A.   No, it is easy. But these men who translated the NEW AMERICAN STANDARD VERSION and especially the NEW INTERNATIONAL VERSION (probably the greatest transgressor-- except for the LIVING VERSION which is far-out) have purposely avoided bringing it over exactly. They don't want that. It's not a question that it is difficult and therefore they cannot succeed. They succeed in the goal they have set for themselves.

Let me show you in the NEW INTERNATIONAL VERSION of 1969, a word on what their goal was (page viii of the Preface):

"The first concern of the translators has been the accuracy of the translation and its fidelity to the THOUGHT of the Biblical writers."

Now, what's wrong with that? Is that what we're interested in, only the THOUGHT? You see, we're interested in the WORDS. We believe in plenary, VERBAL inspiration of Scripture. "Plenary" is "full," (that is, from Genesis to Revelation). "Verbal" means the very words are "God-breathed." If you're only interested in fidelity to the THOUGHT, then you don't care about the WORDS. You can throw this one away, or that one away. And they do. It just grieves me when I look at the NIV.

I listened every morning at 5:45 a.m. to the KING JAMES BIBLE on the cassettes while reading in the NIV to compare the two. How they rend it, twist it, add to it, and move it around! I have finished it finally. I found over **6,653 examples** of DYNAMIC EQUIVALENCY without even half trying. There are many, many more.

The NIV editors **could** have translated the Bible literally, with verbal and formal equivalence, but **they wanted to stay with the THOUGHT, not the WORDS.** To continue reading from the NIV Preface:

> *"They have weighed the significance of the lexical and grammatical details of the Hebrew, Aramaic and Greek texts. At the same time they have striven for MORE THAN a WORD-FOR-**WORD** translation."* [They don't want **WORD-FOR-WORD** translation] *"Because **THOUGHT** patterns and syntax differ from language to language, faithful communication of the **MEANING** of the writers of the Bible **DEMANDS FREQUENT MODIFICATION IN SENTENCE STRUCTURE** and constant regard for the contextual meanings of words."* [NEW INTERNATIONAL VERSION, 1978 edition, p. viii.]

So they have to change the sentence structure, and they do. If it's a question, they often turn it into a statement. If it's a statement, they turn it into a question. Many of the things are backwards. So when you read this, you can see the purpose of it is not to make it exact. They think that is a wrong way to make it. It's not a question of being too difficult.

Let me start from the Hebrew copy. It says *bera-shith*. *b* is "in" and *rashith* is "the head, or beginning." So, Genesis 1:1 says, *"In the beginning God created the heaven and the earth."* The KING JAMES translators wrote, *"In the beginning . . . "* That is a good start, simple, clear, easy. The next word, *bara* "created" *elohim* "God" (the Hebrew has the words in different order) *eth* (the sign of the accusative, or direct object) *ha shamaim* "the heavens" *wa eth* "and" plus the accusative sign again *ha erets* "the earth." This is exactly the way it is. You don't have to change it around.

You will find that the NIV and the others have probably kept this verse just as it is. I'll tell you something about the NIV as well as some of the others. The favorite and the familiar verses they keep pretty well intact in order to sell their Bibles. You turn to Psalm 23 in any of these Bibles they will be very much like the KING JAMES translation because they don't want to take you too far away from what you're used to. They know people look at John 3:16, Psalm 23, Genesis 1:1. The NEW AMERICAN STANDARD has the same rendering of Genesis 1:1. But that doesn't mean that is the way they handle things throughout their translations. They purposely do it.

3.   DO FALSE VERSIONS CONTRIBUTE TO FALSE DOCTRINES?

Q.   Do you think that these new versions lead to groups of people getting off track on the various points of doctrine-- tongues, healings, etc.?
A.   I absolutely do believe they have a part in this. I specifically mention The LIVING VERSION as a version that has been responsible for the increase in the Charismatic Movement, when it comes to their various translations of the tongues chapters, 1 Corinthians 14, etc. They are very free and seem to justify the speaking in tongues and the whole Charismatic Movement. It's so loose and has so many of man's words around God's words, you don't know which are which. Whether these other versions have assisted or not, I don't know. But I know in attending the "Jesus 76" rally (which I attended and recorded in the cow pastures of Pennsylvania) I saw more copies of THE LIVING VERSION than another other version. I saw the boys bare chested, the girls in halters, swimsuits, and scantily clad. I saw kissing, necking, hugging, and lots of strange behavior on the part of young people. But throughout all that, THE LIVING VERSION was used on the platform by these tongues-speakers, Charismatics, Bob Mumford, and all his crowd. They were pushing THE LIVING VERSION as the best translation possible. One of the finest books refuting the LIVING VERSION is our book, THE PARAPHRASED PERVERSION. [B.F.T. #127]. It's an excellent analysis.

4.   WHAT ABOUT "THEE" AND "THOU"?

Q.   What about "thee" and "thou?"
A.   That is another thing. As best I recall, one or two versions say they will refer to Deity and use "Thee" or "Thou," but in referring to humanity they will use "you." In those instances, many times, referring to Jesus they use "you" instead of "Thou" or "Thee." That would be blasphemy against the Lord and disrespect. The KING JAMES BIBLE, in their use of the pronouns, thee, thy, thyself, thou, thine, ye, you, your, and yourselves, have rendered accuracy a great service. All the pronouns beginning with the letter "T" are singular. All the pronouns beginning with the letter "Y" are plural. In this way, the English reader can pick up his KING JAMES BIBLE, and, unlike any of

the other modern versions, he can tell immediately whether the second person pronoun is singular or plural. For example, look at John 3:7:

> *"Marvel not that I said unto thee, Ye must be born again." John 3:7*

If you look at the modern versions, they have the personal pronoun, "you," for both the "thee" and the "ye," thus confusing the meaning. The Lord is using the SINGULAR ("thee") and then the PLURAL ("ye") in the same sentence, and in the same verse, one word right after the other. There are many other instances where the modern versions obscure the true meaning of the English "you." Is it singular or plural? With your KING JAMES BIBLE in hand, you are NEVER left in doubt. And you don't need to know Greek or Hebrew to find out the answer!

5.   WHAT TEXT DOES THE *"OPEN BIBLE"* USE?

Q.   What text does The *Open Bible* use?

A.   At one time, I started to use the *Open Bible* when I compared the Authorized 1611 KING JAMES BIBLE to today's KING JAMES. Suddenly, I came to some words that were spelled differently, so I couldn't make a true comparison. I had to have a standard. For instance, the spelling of "vail." It could be "vail" or "veil." I couldn't tell if it was a change from the original KING JAMES or not. I'm not sure what text they use.

A new Bible has been reprinted. It is NOAH WEBSTER'S VERSION. I haven't analyzed that either. It has been printed by Baker Book House. Webster is the one who compiled the dictionary. He was an excellent man who knew many languages and he worked on the KING JAMES BIBLE. When it came time to clarify certain words, he changed them in his edition of the Bible. It looks fairly good. It is basically the KING JAMES BIBLE except in certain areas where he attempted to clarify some points. It is purported to be the KING JAMES BIBLE.

I have recently been given a NEW KING JAMES VERSION which is called the "OPEN BIBLE" edition. So Nelson publishers really don't mind **which version** of the Bible they call their "OPEN BIBLE."

6.   WHAT STUDY HELPS COULD YOU USE WITH THE KING JAMES BIBLE?

Q.   What would you suggest as a help to use with the KING JAMES BIBLE--one source or two you would use in everyday study?
A.   Strong's Concordance is good. It is keyed to Greek and Hebrew words, and in the back you have the Greek and Hebrew words given in alphabetical order, including the meaning of each word. You would also be helped by a good Bible dictionary. You don't really need much in addition to this in the beginning of your Bible study.

7   IS IT DIFFICULT TO GET THE REAL MEANING IN ENGLISH?

Q.   Isn't it difficult to get the real meaning in the English language?
A.   The English language is a wide and expansive language with technical terms and detailed words from Latin, Greek and all languages. We have a way of saying it in English that many languages do not have. We have a vast number of adjectives, nouns, verbs, etc. that they don't even have in other languages. I would think the English language would be a good one to be able to say exactly what you mean and precisely what is in the Hebrew and Greek.

8.   WHAT ABOUT HEBREW WORDS WITH SEVERAL ENGLISH MEANINGS?

Q.   What about words in the Hebrew that have the meaning of several different words in the English?
A.   There are some words in the Greek and in the Hebrew that have several different nuances, styles, or types of meanings. The job of the translator (as the KING JAMES BIBLE translators have done) is to pick one of those meanings that fits, one of the proper meanings of that word. It is not to change it to some other word that has nothing to do with it. For instance, there is a Hebrew word *beth* which means "house." *Bethel* means "house of God." There's another word in the Hebrew language for temple, *hacol*. Now, *hacol* is "temple" and *beth* is "house." In the NIV, over and over again they say so-and-so built a "temple" when the word is "house." **They don't translate what is there. They change it.**

With the other versions that I analyzed, I didn't have to make so many marks, and I could get through my eighty-five verses a day and finish the Bible in a year. Every time I saw a change I put a red mark and a number. I got clear over to Mark 11 before I found 1,800 serious problems in the NEW AMERICAN STANDARD VERSION. In the NIV, I had already reached over 1,800 serious problems by 2 Samuel. Yet, this is the version that some Fundamentalists of the GENERAL ASSOCIATION OF REGULAR BAPTIST CHURCHES (GARBC) are pushing more than any version we have. Dr. Ernest Pickering was one of the ones pushing it the hardest. He went over to Toledo, as Pastor of the Immanuel Baptist Church, for a few years. I have been told by **reliable witnesses** that one of the things he did was say to his deacons, in effect, "I'm not preaching from the KING JAMES BIBLE any more. I'm going to use the NEW INTERNATIONAL VERSION." They said all right, and they got copies of the NIV and discount NIVs for the people in the pews, and loaded down that large GARBC church with NIVs. Now, I'm an Ohio boy. I was born in Ohio. It is a **sad thing** when an Ohio church, a GARBC church, is packed with the NEW INTERNATIONAL VERSION. **It is a heartache to me.**

I went to Dallas Seminary with Dr. Pickering the entire four years. He was in every required class I sat in--Hebrew, Greek, Theology, and all the others. We were both in the class of 1952. How he can push the NIV, which is so inferior when it comes to the Words of God, is beyond me. Throughout the Old Testament the expression is used, "my own flesh and bones." The word "bone" in Hebrew is *etsem* and "flesh" is *basar*. The NIV renders that expression "flesh and blood." Now, the word "blood" is *dam*, not *etsem*. Blood is blood and bones are bones, and never the two shall meet. But the NIV translators don't care. They're giving the **THOUGHT**. They say, "Those stupid Hebrews, they say `flesh and bones.' Don't they know any better? Don't they know it should be `flesh and blood'"? So we're going to translate it "flesh and blood." They write their own ticket. They have a blank check and anything they want to do, they do it.

The people in the pews, reading the NIV and comparing it to the KING JAMES BIBLE say, "Those silly KING JAMES people, didn't they know any better? Look at this better translation in the NIV." I've heard tell just recently from a dear lady who came to me and said, "My pastor loves the KING JAMES BIBLE, but occasionally he will quote from the NEW INTERNATIONAL VERSION." Now, here's the thing: Whenever someone says, "The KING JAMES BIBLE says this, but the NIV makes it a little plainer," you don't know whether it really is plainer or just a fairy tale, because the

NIV translators don't stick to the **WORDS** of God. **What the NIV says is not necessarily what the Hebrew or Greek says.**

If people want to find out what the Greek or Hebrew says, they can look it up in the Greek or Hebrew Bible, or go to the Strong's Concordance and look at the number in the back and see what the **original word** is and look that up in a Greek or Hebrew lexicon. **You can't trust these versions** because their purpose is not a **WORD-FOR-WORD** translation, but only the **THOUGHT.**

9.   WHY WAS "WINE" USED FOR "GRAPE JUICE" IN THE KING JAMES BIBLE?

Q.   Why did they translate "wine" for what was grape juice? Didn't they have a word for grape juice then? I know that confuses many people today.
A.   The word "wine" is a good English word. If you take the "w" and make it into a "v" it becomes "vine" as in "vineyard." That is all wine is, fruit of the vineyard. The Hebrew word is *yayin* and the Greek word is *oinos*. They both mean "fruit of the vine." We have to interpret the meaning of *yayin* and *oinos* in English. The best book on the subject of wine in the Bible is *Wines in the Bible* by William Patton, which we carry (**B.F.T. #514**), and would recommend it to anyone. What they say in that book is that the Hebrews knew how to keep wines that would not ferment. If you want to have fermented wine, or hard liquor, the words "strong drink" are usually used. Unless it's specifically given by the context, *yayin* in the Hebrew, and *oinos,* in the Greek, always means "unfermented fruit of the vine." Look in a good English dictionary and you will see that "wine" doesn't necessarily always mean an alcoholic beverage, but may merely mean the fruit of the grape.

We have a great many more words that the Hebrews didn't have. We have thousands of entries in the *Third International Webster's Dictionary.* The Hebrew vocabulary is not that extensive. There are fewer words in the Hebrew lexicon than the English. It may be the same for the Greek language. I have Liddell and Scott's classical Greek lexicon which has a sizeable number of terms, more than the Hebrew language has. **Hebrew is a simple,** agricultural or shepherd-type.

10.   IS THE KING JAMES BIBLE WITHOUT TRANSLATION ERRORS OR "INSPIRED"?

Q.   Do you believe the KING JAMES BIBLE to be without translation errors or "inspired"?

A.   Yes, I would say regarding translation errors that I haven't found any either in the Old Testament Hebrew or in the New Testament Greek. I don't like to use the word "inerrant" of any English (or other language) translation of the Bible because the word "inerrant" is implied from the Greek Word, *theopneustos* (2 Timothy 3:16) which means literally, **"GOD-BREATHED."** God Himself did NOT **"BREATHE OUT"** English, or German, or French, or Spanish, or Latin, or Italian. He DID **"BREATHE OUT"** Hebrew/Aramaic, and Greek. Therefore, **ONLY THE HEBREW/ARAMAIC AND GREEK CAN BE RIGHTLY TERMED "GOD-BREATHED" OR "INERRANT," not ANY translation!!** It is my **personal** belief and faith that the HEBREW/ARAMAIC and GREEK TEXTS that underlie the KING JAMES BIBLE have been PRESERVED by God Himself so that these texts can properly be called **"INERRANT"** as well as being the very **"INSPIRED and INFALLIBLE WORDS OF GOD"!! I think that INERRANCY has to do with God's words in the Hebrew/Aramaic and Greek.**

We can't always take over completely 100% what He has there. I think that the KING JAMES translators, when they took the Hebrew or Aramaic, putting it into English, and the Greek, putting it into English, that they matched up one of the Hebrew meanings, or one of the Greek meanings, as they translated into the English language. There are many other choices in English they could have used, but what they did pick was within the rules of both the Hebrew and Greek grammar and English grammar. **Therefore, I have not found any translation errors in the KING JAMES BIBLE, but I do not use "inspired" for it.**

11.   IS "IT" IN ROMANS 8:16 A TRANSLATION ERROR?

Q.   In Romans 8:16 in the NEW KING JAMES the pronoun for the Holy Spirit is translated as "he" but in the KING JAMES it is translated "it." Which is the correct translation?

A.   Strictly speaking, the exact and literal translation is what the KING JAMES translation has, *"itself."* You see, the Holy Spirit in Greek is *to pneuma*, a neuter noun. A neuter noun has pronouns which are also neuter. You have this In Romans 8:16. For instance, it says *touto* (*itself*). The pronoun agrees in gender with the noun. So, *"Spirit itself"* is what is actually in the Greek language.

Now, I don't fault anyone saying that it refers to the Holy Spirit as he expounds or preaches on this passage. The **Person** of the Holy Spirit is "He," but **the form of the Greek noun is a neuter gender.** That would not be considered a translation error because that is exactly what it says.

12.   IS "EASTER" IN ACTS 12:4 A TRANSLATION ERROR?

Q.   In Acts 12:4 the KING JAMES says "Easter," but the NEW KING JAMES renders it as "Passover." That is quite a difference; which one is proper?   From what I understand, Easter is a pagan holiday that didn't come about until later on.
A.   The rendering there is from the Greek text *to pascha* which is "Passover" but that particular Passover was **at the same time** as the Easter festival.   The KJB followed Tyndale and many other translations in rendering this *"EASTER"* in Acts 12:4.

I would recommend two of our publications on this subject. **B.F.T. #1673** by Pastor Raymond Blanton, and **B.F.T. #1737** by Pastor Jack Moorman.   This passover was apparently a travesty on what should have been done at that season and the pagan feast ISHTAR, which is a very pagan feast, was a proper picture for what they were doing. **Now, I take issue with you that Easter is something new.** ISHTAR was a pagan festival which went way back in the Old Testament times to the Phoenician and various pagan cultures.   Ashteroth is the origin of the term Easter--a feminine Baal.   Baal was the male and Ashteroth the female.   That is one translation some have asked about, and I would say certainly that "passover" would not be a wrong rendering; yet since they were carrying on as they were, "Easter" would be a good rendering also because it was at the same time. As you know, our pagan feast of Easter and our festival of Easter, with the egg-rolling and other things, is extremely pagan.   There is no question about it.   It occurs on or about the time of the Jewish Passover.   For more details, consult the above-mentioned articles that take this issue up in detail.   If you notice the context of Acts 12:4, you'll notice in verse 3 that "then were the days of UNLEAVENED   BREAD."   If   you   remember,   the   date   of "UNLEAVENED BREAD" as specified in Leviticus 23:6, was the "fifteenth day" of the first month.   In Leviticus 23:5, the date for the "PASSOVER" was the "fourteenth day" of the first month.   In Acts 12:4, we read the words: "intending after Easter (or Passover) to bring him forth to the people."   If it was already the "DAYS OF UNLEAVENED

BREAD" or the **15th** of the month, how could the **14th** of the month come AFTER the **15th**? This would be the case if this were the normal "Passover."

13. WHAT ABOUT LUKE 1:18?

Q. **In Luke 1:14 you were talking about Zacharias and his wife being old and stricken in age; could it be that the Lord wanted to be sure that THIS wife was meant since it was the custom of that time to have more than one wife?**
A. No. I don't believe this is the reason for it. I believe the Lord is speaking of Zacharias' wife in two different ways-- both *"old"* and *"stricken in age."* I believe he had only one wife. They were both old, and this was a child of their old age. God knew what He wanted to say and neither of the words should be omitted.

14. WHAT ABOUT THE FOOTNOTES IN THE NEW KING JAMES VERSION?

Q. **You said the footnotes in the NEW KING JAMES were confusing but weren't they just the original Greek?**

A. No, the footnotes represent the Nestle/United Bible Society text ["NU"] and not the Greek of the *Received Text.* The Nestle/United Bible Society text ["NU"] is the one the liberals believe, and many Fundamentalists believe, is the best Greek text--the *Nestle/Aland 26th Edition.* The Nestle & United Bible Society have united on this one edition. It differs from the *Textus Receptus* that underlies our KING JAMES BIBLE over **5,600 times**, involving **9,970 Greek words.** The footnotes are confusing because to the young believer, or even an older believer, it causes doubt as to what is the Words of God. For instance, in the communion service, when your pastor is trying to read from 1 Corinthians 11:24, *". . . this is my body which is **BROKEN** for you."* The SCOFIELD VERSION in the margin casts doubt upon the word *"broken."* They want to take it out. I'm against the Scofield note in that particular instance. The word *"broken"* is in the Greek language, in the Textus Receptus--there is no doubt about it. The NEW KING JAMES VERSION has the same doubt about that particular place and has a footnote. "The Nestle/United Bible Society omits `broken.'" Here you have a new believer (or older believer) reading his NEW KING JAMES VERSION, and there's doubt cast on the authenticity of the words of God during the communion service.   In addition to the "NU" footnotes which represent the Westcott-and-Hort-type of text, there is the letter "M" which refers, when used, to the so-called "majority text" of Hodges and Farstad which departs from the *Textus Receptus.* **B.F.T. #1617** is a 160-page analysis which thoroughly disputes the truthfulness of this so-called "majority text."   It is by Dr. Jack A. Moorman. You may also get a short refutation of this so-called "majority text" by writing for **B.F.T. #1448** by yours truly. It is entitled, *DEFECTS IN THE SO-CALLED 'MAJORITY GREEK TEXT.'* There is another booklet that is helpful in all of this question. It is a small, yet valuable pamphlet condensing Dr. Moorman's longer book by yours truly. It is entitled, *"WHY REJECT THE SO-CALLED 'MAJORITY' TEXT."* It is **B.F.T. #1727.**

15.   WHY ARE THERE SO MANY OTHER VERSIONS OTHER THAN THE KING JAMES BIBLE?

Q.   Why do they have these other versions? Why didn't they stick to the KING JAMES BIBLE?
          A.   The translation business is a business. **The translation of the Bible, I believe, should be in the hands of the local churches.** Churches are the ones who should produce the Words of God. They did produce it in KING JAMES' day. It was the Puritans and the Anglicans, the Church of England, that got together and with the authority of KING JAMES--yet **it was the churches, not the publishing house,** that got this Bible together. **It's the publishing houses that**

Order Blank

Name:_____

Address:_____

City & State:_____Zip:_____

Credit Card
#:_____Expires:_____

Latest Books

[ ] Send 2 Timothy--Preaching Verse by Verse, by Pastor D. A. Waite, 250 pages, hardback ($11+$5 S&H) fully indexed.
[ ] Send *A Critical Answer to God's Word Preserved* by Pastor D. A. Waite, 192 pp. perfect bound ($11.00+$4.00 S&H)

The Most Recently Published Books

[ ] Send *8,000 Differences Between Textus Receptus & Critical Text* by Dr. J. A. Moorman, 544 pp., hd.back ($20+$5+ S&H)
[ ] *Early Manuscripts, Church Fathers, & the Authorized Version* by Dr. Jack Moorman, $18+$5 S&H. Hardback
[ ] Send *The LIE That Changed the Modern World* by Dr. H. D. Williams ($16+$5 S&H) Hardback book
[ ] Send *With Tears in My Heart* by Gertrude G. Sanborn. Hardback 414 pp. ($25+$5 S&H) 400 Christian Poems

Preaching Verse by Verse Books

[ ] Send 1 Timothy--Preaching Verse by Verse, by Pastor D. A. Waite, 288 pages, hardback ($11+$5 S&H) fully indexed.
[ ] Send *Romans--Preaching Verse by Verse* by Pastor D. A. Waite 736 pp. Hardback ($25+$5 S&H) fully indexed
[ ] Send *Colossians & Philemon--Preaching Verse by Verse* by Pastor D. A. Waite ($12+$5 S&H) hardback, 240 pages.
[ ] Send *Philippians--Preaching Verse by Verse* by Pastor D. A. Waite ($10+$5 S&H) hardback, 176 pages.
[ ] Send *Ephesians--Preaching Verse by Verse* by Pastor D. A. Waite ($12+$5 S&H) hardback, 224 pages.
[ ] Send *Galatians--Preaching Verse By Verse* by Pastor D. A. Waite ($12+$5 S&H) hardback, 216 pages.

Send or Call Orders to:
THE BIBLE FOR TODAY
900 Park Ave., Collingswood, NJ 08108
Phone: 856-854-4452; FAX:--2464; Orders: 1-800 JOHN 10:9
E-Mail Orders: BFT@BibleForToday.org; Credit Cards OK

ABOUT THE AUTHOR

The author of this booklet, Dr. D. A. Waite, received a B.A. (Bachelor of Arts) in classical Greek and Latin from the University of Michigan in 1948, a Th.M. (Master of Theology), with high honors, in New Testament Greek Literature and Exegesis from Dallas Theological Seminary in 1952, and M.A. (Master of Arts) in Speech from Southern Methodist University in 1953, a Th.D. (Doctor of Theology), with honors, in Bible Exposition from Dallas Theological Seminary in 1955, and a Ph.D. in Speech from Purdue University in 1961. He holds both New Jersey and Pennsylvania teacher certificates in Greek and Language Arts.

He has been a teacher in the areas of Greek, Hebrew, Bible, Speech, and English for over thirty-five years in nine schools, including one junior high, one senior high, three Bible institutes, two colleges, two universities, and one seminary. He served his country as a Navy Chaplin for five years on active duty; pastured two churches; was Chairman and Director of the Radio and Audio-Film Commission of the American Council of Christian Churches; since 1971, has been Founder, President, and Director of THE BIBLE FOR TODAY; since 1978, has been President of the DEAN BURGON SOCIETY; has produced over 700 other studies, booklets, cassettes, or VCR's on various topics; and is heard on a thirty-minute weekly radio program IN DEFENSE OF TRADITIONAL BIBLE TEXTS on radio, shortwave, and streaming on the internet at BibleForToday.org, 24/7/365. Dr. and Mrs. Waite have been married since 1948; they have four sons, one daughter, and, at present, eight grandchildren and six great-grandchildren. Since October 4, 1998 he has been Pastor of 𝔅ible 𝔉or 𝔗oday 𝔅aptist 𝔠hurch in Collingswood, New Jersey.

Breinigsville, PA USA
21 September 2010
245538BV00007B/1/P

9 781568 480060